Dan Taylor

A Dissertation on Singing in the Worship of God

Interspersed with occasional strictures on Mr. Boyce's late tract

Dan Taylor

A Dissertation on Singing in the Worship of God
Interspersed with occasional strictures on Mr. Boyce's late tract

ISBN/EAN: 9783337290597

Printed in Europe, USA, Canada, Australia, Japan

Cover: Foto ©Lupo / pixelio.de

More available books at **www.hansebooks.com**

ON

SINGING

IN THE

WORSHIP OF GOD:

Interfperfed with Occafional STRICTURES

ON

Mr. BOYCE's late TRACT,

ENTITLED,

" SERIOUS THOUGHTS on the prefent
" Mode and Practice of SINGING in the
" public Worfhip of God."

By DAN TAYLOR.

" The prefent practice of SINGING in public Wor-
" fhip, either is, or is not, an error : if it is not,
" I hope our Brethren, who plead for, and practife
" it, will be kind enough, at leaft, to endeavour to
" prove it a truth ; as it certainly belongs to them
" fo to do."
SERIOUS THOUGHTS, Page 5.

Printed for the Author ; and Sold by J. BUCKLAND,

Paternofter-Row, and J. MORTOM, No. 187,
High-Holborn.

TO THE

Reverend Mr. BOYCE.

SIR,

WHEN I had heard of your intention to write and publiſh againſt finging the praiſes of God in divine worſhip, I was very averſe to taking up my pen on that ſubject ; though I was much ſolicited to do it, by ſeveral of my friends. I had many reaſons for this, which I need not now to name. And when I received and read your tract on the ſubject, which was

fome

some time after its publication, ; I had one reason more added to the former: it was this ; I was afraid, from the cast and contents of it, lest I should not be able to do justice to what I apprehended to be the truth ; and yet to manifest a proper degree of respect to the " hoary head ; especially when found " in the way of righteousness." But, when in a few days after, I received your last private letter, on the 23d of December, for reasons derived from that, which you will easily judge of the force of, when you recollect what your letter c ontained ; I came to a resolution to put together a few thoughts ; and, if I heard of nothing printed, or designed by any other, I would put them to the press. Accordingly, I now send them abroad ; with earnest and repeated prayers, that, by the blessing of God, they may contribute to his glory, the discovery of truth, and the establishment of any who waver; or the conviction of any who err, respecting the practice in question. I did not think it necessary or proper

proper to go regularly through your piece, and take it in courfe; as this might lead to fome perfonal reflections. I mean chiefly, on thofe large parts of your tract which are fo evidently addreffed to the paffions rather than the judgment. Nor did your requifitions at the beginning and end of your tract, feem to require me to take this method. I am not confcious, however, of having omitted any thing that is properly argumentative. Such as my performance is, I pray that the blefling of God may attend the reading of it, for the purpofes defigned; and am,

Dear Sir,

Your affectionate Brother,

In the bonds of the Gofpel,

DAN TAYLOR.

Turvile Street,
Jan. 7, 1786.

A DIS.

A

DISSERTATION, &c.

I. TO SING is to pronounce *musically*, by modulating the voice, and proportioning the founds of the fyllables to one another; in fuch a manner as may be harmonious, and pleafant to the hearer. And to fing the praifes of God, is to *pronounce* the praifes of God in this harmonious manner. Thus it is different from fpeaking; from prayer; from giving thanks; from joy and thankfulnefs of heart; and from every other operation both of mind and tongue in which there is no fuch melody. Thus it is underftocd in common life; and this is undeniably the meaning of the word in fcripture; both in our Englifh verfion, and in the original languages; as can eafily be evinced, if neceffary. But Mr. BOYCE feems not to difpute this; and, therefore, I at prefent take it for granted as what is on both fides allowed,

II. SING-

II. SINGING the praises of God, is plainly and frequently recommended in the sacred scriptures, " Sing unto the Lord, for he hath triumphed " gloriously.—Sing praises to the Lord, which " dwelleth in Zion.—Sing unto the Lord, O ye " saints of his; and give thanks at the remem- " brance of his holiness.—Sing unto him with the " psaltry, and an instrument of ten strings.—Sing " unto him a new song; play skilfully with a loud " voice.—Sing praises to God, sing praises; sing " praises unto our king, sing praises: for God " is the king of all the earth: sing ye praises with " understanding.—Make a joyful noise unto God, " all ye lands: sing forth the honour of his name: " make his praise glorious.—O let the nations be " glad, and sing for joy. — Sing unto God, sing " praises to his name; extol him that rideth upon " the heavens, by his name JAH, and rejoice before " him.—Sing aloud unto God our strength: make " a joyful noise unto the God of Jacob.—O come " let us sing unto the Lord, let us make a joyful " noise unto the rock of our salvation. Let us " come before his presence with thankgiving, " and make a joyful noise unto him with psalms. " —O sing unto the Lord a new song: sing unto " the Lord all the earth: sing unto the Lord, " bless his name; shew forth his salvation from " day to day.—Make a joyful noise unto the " Lord, all ye lands: serve the Lord with glad- " ness; come before his presence with singing.— " Sing unto him, sing psalms unto him: talk ye of " all his wonderous works.—Praise ye the Lord, " for the Lord is good: sing praises unto his " name, for it is pleasant.—Praise ye the Lord; " for it is good to sing praises unto the Lord ;
" for

" for it is pleafant; and praife is comely.—*Sing*
" unto the Lord with thankfgiving; *fing* praife
" upon the harp unto our God.—*Sing* unto the
" Lord a new *fong*, and his praife in the congre-
" gation of the faints.—*Sing* unto the Lord, for
" he hath done excellent things : this is known
" in all the earth.—*Sing* unto the Lord a new
" *fong*; and his praife from the end of the earth.
" —Let the wildernefs, and the cities thereof,
" lift up their voices : the villages that Kedar
" doth inhabit.—Let the inhabitants of the rock
" *fing*, let them *fhout* from the tops of the moun-
" tains.——Speaking to yourfelves in *pfalms* and
" *hymns*, and fpiritual *fongs*, *finging*, and making
" melody in your hearts to the Lord.—Let
" the word of Chrift dwell in you richly, in
" all wifdom ; teaching and admonifhing one
" another in *pfalms*, and *hymns*, and fpiritual
" *fongs* ; *finging* with grace in your hearts to
" the Lord.—Is any among you afflicted ? let
" him pray. Is any merry ? let him *fing pfalms*."
See Exod. xv. 21. Pfal. ix. 11. xxx. 4. xxxiii.
2, 3. xlvii. 6, 7. lxvi. 1, 2. lxvii. 4. lxviii. 4.
lxxxi. 1. xcv. 1, 2. xcvi. 1, 2. c. 1, 2. cv. 2.
cxxxv. 3. cxlvii. 1, 7. cxlvix. 1. Ifa. xii. 5. xlii.
10, 11. Ephef. v. 19. Col. iii. 16. James v. 13.
  Thus it appears, that finging to the Lord, and
finging his praifes, is frequently and warmly recommended in that book, which I readily allow,
as well as Mr. B. is " the only rule of our faith
" and practice in all things of a purely religious
nature§." Mr. B. takes a great deal of pains to addrefs our paffions ; but very little to inform our

§ Serious Thoughts, page 5.

underftandings ; which, with fubmiffion, is not,
I think, very laudable in matters of controverfy.
It may impofe upon the ignorant, and terrify the
timorous, and the tender confcience, as the Bulls
of the Pope, and the Anathemas of Athanafius,
alfo do ; but it will never fettle the mind on the
firm bafis of infallible truth. He fays a great
deal, in his way, about " anfwering it to God at
" laft,"—" venturing on as we do,"—" being
" firmly eftablifhed in this pleafing error," about
" anfwering for this in the lower court of con-
" fcience, and the fupreme above, " &c. &c.
&c.‡ But, in my opinion, this might have been
all very well fpared, with little difadvantage to
his caufe, till we had acknowledged our error,
and confeffed ourfelves wrong. He fpeaks rather
tauntingly of " *finging* God's praifes," and " RE-
" MINDS us," how we " all open our mouths to-
" gether to *fing* God's praifes ; as we call it :"
which appears a little more ludicrous than might
have been expected. And, if I had not known
the author, I fhould probably have called it *pro-
fane* ; becaufe thefe are not the words of men,
but of God himfelf ; and therefore demand our
reverence. For proof of which I refer the reader
to the collection of fcriptures, which I have
made above ; and many more, fome of which
may be cited in the following pages. I only
here obferve, that the *manner* of finging may be
confidered afterwards. With regard to the practice itfelf, I beg leave to afk Mr. Boyce two
queftions.

1. As

‡ P. 21, 33, &c.

1. As it is evident this practice is fo much recommended in the infpired volume ; is it not the duty of thofe who chufe to oppofe it, to fhew where it is abrogated, and where the bleffed God has appointed it to be laid afide ? 2. If this cannot be done, whether it is not more becoming a Chriftian, to perform it as well as he can, than to pafs it over in neglect ? And may not the fame be faid of Chriftian *churches*, as of individuals ; efpecially as thefe injunctions and recommendations of the practice are addreffed to churches, as well as individuals ?

III. *Singing* the praifes of God is not only frequently recommended in fcripture ; but it is recommended as an *excellent* practice too.—And this, not only in the judgment of carnal men, but of God himfelf ; that is, of thofe who fpoke by the Spirit of God.——And great numbers have experienced the truth of it. " Praife the " Lord ; for the Lord is good : *fing* praifes unto " his name, for it is PLEASANT. It is a *good* " thing to give thanks unto the Lord ; and to " *fing* praifes unto thy name, O thou moft High. " Praife ye the Lord ; for it is *good* to *fing* " praifes unto our God ; for it is *pleafant* ; and " praife is comely." Pfal. xcii. 1. cxxxv. 3. cxlvii. 1. I forbear to amplify and enlarge upon thefe feveral expreffions, for the fake of brevity. It is enough that we have the teftimony of him, who " knows what is in man ;" to the *comelinefs*, the *pleafantnefs*, the *goodnefs* of *finging* our great Creator's praifes. I alfo omit thofe paffages of the *New* Teftament (Ephef. v. 19. Col. iii. 16.) in which the apoftle informs us, that we receive mutual *inftruction* and *admonition*

in

in this facred and delightful exercife ; becaufe, my friend, and I yet differ with regard to the meaning of thofe paffages, and their authenticity in favour of the practice of *finging* in Chriftian worfhip. I alfo here omit all remarks arifing from the nature of man, and the effects that melody confeffedly has upon the human mind ; though thefe would help to demonftrate the wifdom and goodnefs of God, in recommending to us this facred exercife. Thefe things I pafs by, becaufe I wifh to proceed on fure and *uncontefted* ground ; and to leave as little rcom as I can for quarrel and altercation. Suffice it then, to fay here, that God himfelf fets his own *probatum eft* to the goodnefs and pleafantnefs of *finging* the praifes of his great name.

Mr. B. takes much pains to perfuade us that this practice is of no ufe‡ : But he muft allow us to prefer the judgment of an all-wife God, to that of fallible men. He very gravely tells his *finging brethren*, that he, " don't fee wherein they " are more holy, more heavenly-minded, &c." which, indeed, has nothing to do with the prefent difpute : but if it had, Mr. B. undoubtedly takes an effectual method not to be confuted : for he can never think his finging brethren will boaft of their improvement in grace and holinefs; and pretend, that they are in thefe fuperior to others. And if this muft be determined by examining all the hearts and all the lives of thofe who do fing, and thofe who do not ; which is the only method I can think of: then, to be fure, the debate could not be brought to an iffue

‡ P. 27, 30, 51.

in this age, nor the next. " The judgment of the great day" alone can decide this queſtion. Should the people commonly called Quakers argue in this manner with the Baptiſts reſpecting Baptiſm and the Lord's ſupper, for inſtance; *their* arguments would appear to Mr. B. in their proper colours of ridicule and contempt. The queſtion is, does God *approve* of the practice ? The anſwer is, he *recommends* it, becauſe it is *good* and *pleaſant.* And therefore, however abuſed by ſome, or however unprofitable to others ; it ought to be attended to.

I venture to add, that what the bleſſed God here declares to be the excellency of ſinging his praiſes, great numbers have happily proved by experience; and thouſands now alive can, without any heſitation ſet their ſeal to it, as well as in former ages. Not a few have known it to contribute greatly to their converſion to God. I could mention ſome of their names, if needful and proper. And great numbers more have proved its influence and advantage in their progreſs in grace and holineſs. How St Auſtin, Beza, Luther, and others, of equal learning and piety have atteſted the comfort, ſupport, and ſpiritual advantage they have received by this ſacred exerciſe, is well known. But the brevity I aim at, forbids me to tranſcribe their words. In ſhort, I am well perſuaded, that few have ſincerely attended to this *good work,* who have not proved the benefit of it : and who are not able by experience, as well as in faith, to ſay, " It is a good thing to give thanks unto " the Lord, and to ſing praiſes unto thy name, " O Moſt High !"

B   IV.

IV. SINGING the praifes of God is an ancient practice, and fo far as we can find, has been continued from age to age; though it may not have been univerfally practifed.

That this was the practice of good men, under the Old Teftament, will not be denied by any who believe the fcriptures. The evidences of it are fo numerous, and fo clear, that it would be equally tedious and unneceffary here to adduce them. The whole book of Pfalms, and many parts of the Old Teftament hiftory, make it undeniable. Nor am I able to recollect any evidence, from the little knowledge I have of antiquity, that it was ever laid afide, or the practice of it difcarded in the New Teftament Church. But that our Saviour and his apoftles, and, at leaft the Churches at Corinth, Ephefus, and Colofs practifed it, is allowed by Mr. B. himfelf. See his Tract, at large.

Mr. B. prefixes to his performance, what he calls, " a word of intelligence ;" which is defigned, as may be fuppofed, to perfuade his readers that finging was not practifed in the primitive ages of Chriftianity. But whoever will be at the pains to examine the early writers of antiquity, fuch as Juftin Martyr, Tertullian, Origin, Cyprian, &c. will find fufficient proof of the contrary‡. I beg leave to give one citation only, from *Tertullian*, who flourifhed about
A. D.

‡ Thofe who are not able, or not willing to confult the *Fathers*, may read Dr. Gill's Sermon on 1 Cor. xiv. 15. Bingham's Antiquities, B. 14. chap. 1. p. 661. Folio edit. 1726. and Sir Peter King's Inquiry. Part 2. chap. 1. &c.

A. D. 200. Speaking of the Chriſtian worſhip, he mentions theſe four parts : Reading the ſcriptures; ſinging of Pſalms, preaching Sermons, and Prayer§. One of our ableſt writers, therefore ſays, " We affirm that plain ſinging has been in uſe, from the beginning of the Church, and is grounded upon the example of our Saviour, and the command of his apoſtles‖." And to me it is wonderful that any man of reading ſhould deny it.

Our Author ſays, " The practice of ſinging in the public worſhip of God, if I miſtake not, was introduced and ſet up in the baptized churches, by Mr. B. Keach, and Mr. W. Allen, in the laſt century : Such a practice having been never known among them before‡." I venture to aſk my aged friend, what kind of churches were the Chriſtian Churches in the time of Tertullian ? Were not they baptized churches ? A man muſt have a good deal of aſſurance, who would undertake to prove, that there were at that time, any other than baptized churches. And yet at that time the Scriptures were read, " and Pſalms ſung," in the " public worſhip " of God."

That ſinging in the worſhip of God was the practice of the following ages, I ſuppoſe Mr. B. will not deny. That ſinging the praiſes of God

B 2   was

---

§ Jam vero prout ſcripturæ leguntur, aut Pſalmi canuntur, aut adlocutiones proferuntur, aut petitiones delegantur, &c. De Anima, cap. ix. p 270. Edit. 1675.

‡ Pierce's Vindication of the Diſſeneers, Part III. Chap. 3.

† P. 5.

was much practised by the chief instruments in the reformation, and that it was a great mean of promoting the Reformation too, is well known. I think it may not be inconsistent with my intended brevity, to transcribe a few lines from that most laborious writer, Mr. John Quick†, "It " was the great care of the first reformers to " preach up sound doctrine, to institute and cele- " cebrate pure evangelical worship, and to restore " the ancient primitive discipline. They set up " purity of worship, according to the scripture " rule.—The holy bible is read in their solemn " meetings, in the great congregations.—*Clement Marot*, a courtier, and a great wit, was " advised by Mr. *Vatablus*, Regius Professor of " the Hebrew tongue in the university of *Paris*, " to consecrate his muse to God ; which coun- " sel he embraceth, and translateth fifty of Da- " vid's psalms into French metre. Mr. Beza did " the other hundred, and all the scripture songs. " *Lewis Guaimel*, another Asaph or Jeduthun, " a most skilful master of music, set those sweet " and melodious tunes, unto which they are " sung, even unto this day. This holy ordi- " nance charmed the ears, hearts, and affections " of court and city, town and country. They " were sung in the *Louvre*, as well as in the *Pres* " *des Clerks*, by the ladies, princes, yea, and by " Henry the Second himself. This one ordi- " nance only, contributed mightily to the down- " fal of popery, and the propagation of the gos- " pel." This is one, among many testimonies, of the usefulness of singing psalms; and the regard

† Synodicon in Gallia Reformata, Vol I. p. 5. 1692.

-paid

paid to it at the Reformation, not only in France, but also in England, and other parts, where the Reformation was carried on with vigour and success. Let it be granted, that this (as well as other ordinances) is misimproved, and abused by wicked men. That can be no reason for laying it aside, unless we are to lay all ordinances aside for the same reason. I am mistaken, if it will not be found, on examination, that whenever the Lord has revived his work in any particular manner, either in the hearts of his people, or in the conversion of sinners; this practice has been revived at the same time. Nor is this to be at all wondered at, because it is a practice peculiarly suitable to the disposition of one who is truly alive to God. This is manifest, not only by constant experience and observation; but also by the general tenor of the Book of Psalms, and many historical anecdotes in the Old Testament; and by Acts xvi. 25. and James v. 13, in the New Testament.

Mr. B. however, seems to lay some stress on the *date* of singing in the *baptized churches*. For he not only tells us, at the beginning of his tract, that Mr. Keach and Mr. Allen introduced it among them; but afterwards calls it a " new " invention;" a " new invented way, &c*." How far this may work on the prejudices and passions of the unthoughtful, the end it is particularly calculated to serve; I presume not to say. But it puts me in mind of the ingenuity of some other controvertists on other subjects. The Papists cry to the Protestants, " Where was

* P. 5, 30, 34.

your

your doctrine before Luther ?" And the pœdo-
baptifts would difcard the Baptifts by deriving
their practice from *Munfter*, and dating it about
1532. They are both properly anfwered, "the
" Proteftant doctrine, and that of Believers Bap-
" tifm, are contained in the bible, and were re-
" ceived in the churches, from Chrift and his
" apoftles many ages before Luther was born ;
" before the troubles at Munfter ; and be-
" fore the commencement of the fixteenth cen-
" tury." The fame anfwer will ferve here. The
practice of " finging pfalms, and hymns, and
fpiritual fongs," not only was recommended by
the apoftles, and abundantly enforced by precept and example in the Old and New Teftament ; but was received from the apoftles,
and practifed in the firft ages of the Chriftian
church fifteen hundred years before Mr. Keach
and Mr. Allen came into exiftence. The tefti-
monies of Pliny, the Heathen, and the early
writers of the church above-mentioned, are in-
conteftible proofs of this.

This appears to be a proper place to anfwer a
Query, which has often been propofed ; and feems
with fome, a matter of great importance : the
query is, "In what manner did the ancients Chrif-
" tians perform this fervice?" I venture to anfwer
" in the words of the learned and indefatigable
Bingham ; who refers to many ancient writers
in proof of what he afferts. " (1) Sometimes
" the *pfalms* were fung by one perfon alone ; the
" reft hearing only with attention. (2.) Some-
" times they were fung by the whole affembly,
" joining all together. (3.) Sometimes alter-
" nately, by the congregation divided into dif-
" tinct

" tinct quires; the one part repeating one verse,
" the other another. (4.) Sometimes one person
" repeated the firſt part of the verſe, and the reſt
" joining altogether in the cloſe of it‖."

As Mr. Boyce's inſinuations, concerning the
novelty of ſinging in the baptized churches, will,
I am perſuaded, have much influence on the
minds of weak people, different ways ; I beg the
reader's patience a little longer on this ſubject.
When this practice is called, " a new inven-
" tion," among them, &c. the ignorant reader,
may be led to conclude, that the baptiſts had
worſhipped God publickly, as a ſeparate community, in this nation, long before ſinging was
begun ; and that in compariſon of that time, the
buſineſs of ſinging is but of very ſhort duration. But theſe ſhould conſider, that though
there is good reaſon to believe there were always thoſe in the chriſtian church who ad-
hered to, and ſteadily maintained the doctrine
and practice of believer's Baptiſm ; yet we have
no evidence, that I know of, that they ſeparated
themſelves from others, and ſet up the public
worſhip of God, and formed churches among

* Antiquities, B. xiv. ch. 1. p. 665. The reader,
however, ſhould here be apprized, that Antiphonous
ſinging, or ſinging by turns, does not appear to be
as early as the apoſtolic age. Hiſtorians differ about
the time when it was introduced. *Socrates* places it
ſoon after the apoſtles ; in the days of *Ignatius. Theo-
dorit*, in the fourth century. The ſubject is diſcuſſed
by Mr. *Pierce.*

Vindication of the Diſſenters, Part 3. chap. 3,
pages 101, 102.

was

themfelves, as a diftinct body, till pretty far in the laft century; and not long before finging was introduced among them. It is certain, indeed, there were fome Baptifts in England at the very dawn of the Reformation from Popery: and thirty-one of them, who fled from *England*, were put to death at *Delft*, in the year 1539; the men were beheaded, and the women drowned[*]. And two Baptifts were burnt in Smithfield about the fame time[‡]. But the Baptifts continued almoft one hundred years after that time, in communion with other churches, labouring to promote the Reformation, and to reduce religious matters to the only proper ftandard, *the word of God*; which priefts and princes oppofed, and endeavoured to prevent. And all this time they were perfecuted in a manner, which fhocks humanity to relate. It does not appear, that they began to form feparate focieties for public worfhip, till about the year 1633, or afterwards [‖]: fo that till this period we have no accounts of the pub-
" lic worfhip of the Baptized churches[†].

Now

* Brandt's Hift. of the Reformation, Vol. I. p. 77.
‡ Fuller's Church Hiftory, Book iv.
‖ Nr. Neal fays, 1640. But in this, and fome other hints concerning the Baptifts, he appears not to have been fufficiently accurate. Compare Neal's Hiftory of the Puritans, Vol. ii. p. 392. Hiftory of Religion, Vol. iv. p. 200. Crofby's Hiftory of the Baptifts, Vol. i. p. 148.
§ I obferve here, by the way, that left any fhould be weak enough to afperfe the Baptifts as a *novel* fect, which has fometimes been inadvertently done; they ought to remember, that the firft *Independent* church in England was only founded in the year 1616: and

. the

Now Mr. Keach was born in 1640, and wrote in favour of *singing* in the year 1691, at moſt not ſixty years after the firſt Baptiſt church was founded in England : and now almoſt a hundred years ago : and if we conſider how many errors in circumſtantials there were among the Baptiſts, as well as other parties, at their firſt emerging from Popiſh darkneſs;—how full the nation was of Popery; even at that time ;—how much difficulty, and what ſufferings they underwent to maintain their ground in more fundamental matters ; how much they were tormented and grieved with unmeaning *Antiphonias* ;—and how ſtrong human prejudices generally are ;—it is no wonder to me that they they did not ſooner enquire into, and more readily embrace this ſacred practice ; or that many oppoſed it; even after that good man had written in favour of it. On the whole, however, it is neither the novelty nor the antiquity of any practice, that proves it right or wrong ; but it's conformity with the ſcripture, or the contrary.

(V.) *Singing* the praiſes of God was not peculiar to the Jewiſh diſpenſation; but is equally proper, if not more ſo under the goſpel. By ſome of Mr. B's expreſſions, one would almoſt think he meant to conſider it as merely a Jewiſh ordinance ; though I confeſs he is not explicit on this head. That it was enjoined and practiſed among the Jews he will not deny. Now if he with us to conſider it as *confined* to

the *Baptiſts* being independents, in point of church government, had fellowſhip with them, till 1633. See Neal's Hiſtory, Vol. ii. p. 108.

that

that difpenfation, I think he fhould have proved that it *ought* to be fo confined. But this he has not done ; nor do I think this can be proved. On the contrary, feveral arguments may be offered for the continuance of this practice to the end of time. I mention the following.

We have no account of the inftitution of it among the pofitive rites of the Jews, as, if it had been peculiar to that difpenfation, might naturally have been expected. Though I do not pretend that this argument is abfolutely decifive ; yet it carries fome probability in it. And, I add,

We have no intimation that finging was to be laid afide with the Jewifh Œconomy ; which is at leaft, an argument equally probable in favor of it's being an ordinance continuing through the chriftian difpenfation. It was practifed by good men, before the Jewifh law was given, Exod. xv. It is not any where mentioned among the Jewifh pofitive inftitutes. The pfalmift calls upon the heathens, upon all nations, and all lands to praife the Lord, Pf. lxvi. lxvii. xcvi. And the heathen nations did, in fact, practife this, as their writings teftify*.— The angels practifed it at the creation, Job xxxviii. 6, 7. And it will be the work of faints and angels in heaven, for ever.

The pfalmift himfelf confiders it not only as different from, but fuperior to Jewifh facrifices ; and more pleafing to God than they are, Pf. lxix.

---

* See Dr. GILL's Sermon, 1 Cor. xiv. 15. where feveral of thefe thoughts are illuftrated more largely.

lxix. 30, 31—And the New Teſtament is not only ſilent with reſpect to the abolition of it; but inculcates and enforces it both by precept and example, Matt. xxvi. 30. Mark xiv. 26. Acts xvi. 25. 1 Cor. xiv. 15. Ephes. v. 19. Col. iii. 16. Jam. v. 13. Can we reaſonably ſuppoſe all this to be leſs than a certain proof, that ſinging the praiſes of God is to be conſidered as a branch of natural religion, a part of moral duty ; and to be continued in the church as a part of New Teſtament worſhip ?

I think it would be eaſy to prove that many prophecies foretell that the chriſtian church would ſing the praiſes of God, and that in the moſt literal ſenſe, as Pſ. xlvii, xlviii. xcv. Iſ. xxxv. li. lii. &c. But, as this would require ſome labour and time ; and more eaſily admit the quibbles of an adverſary, I forego the advantage, and here farther add, ,that ſinging is evidently a goſpel ordinance, becauſe the apoſtle is par-ticularly careful to inculcate the practice even in thoſe very epiſtles, where he ſhews that the Jewiſh ceremonial laws and rites are abro-gated. Compare Eph. ii. 14, 15. Col. ii. 14. 16, 17. 20. where he profeſſedly ſpeaks of the abrogation of Jewiſh ceremonies, with Epheſ. v 19. Col. iii. 16. Where he profeſſedly inculcates and enforces the 'practice of ſinging. Now can we imagine the apoſtle would in this manner diſcard Jewiſh ceremonies, and enjoin ſinging, if both ſtood on the ſame ground ? If ſinging were not deſigned to be a continued practice, even when Jewiſh ceremonies are all ended ?

Beſides,

Befides, does not finging anfwer the fame moral purpofes ftill, as it did under the law? Hath it not all the *goodnefs* and *pleafantnefs* in it now, that it had in the days of Mofes and David? Why then fhould it be laid afide under the gofpel?

Again, I beg leave farther to add, I could never yet fee that nearly the fame arguments may not be ufed againft praying or preaching under the New teftament, as againft finging.

I venture here to afk, Mr. B. a few queftions, Are not both praying, preaching, and finging commanded under the New Teftament, as well as under the Old; and one as exprefsly as the other? Are they not all enjoined by the fame authority? May they not all be performed by wicked men? Are there any *particular* directions given concerning the *manner* of preaching and praying in the New Teftament, more than concerning the *manner* of finging? Are there not fufficient *general* directions given concerning the *manner* of praying and preaching? Of the *manner* of finging we may enquire again by and by. I add; Do prayer and preaching anfwer valuable ends for the inftruction and admonition of men? And is it not plain, from Col. iii. 16. that finging does fo too? And, though a few receive not this benefit on account of their prejudices; yet have not thoufands and millions teftified the truth of it from their own experience?

VI. Mr. B. feems fometimes to object abfolutely againft all finging in publick worfhip*. Sometimes he appears only to militate againft " fuch a fort of finging as we practife in our

churches

* P. 5. &c.

churches§." He frankly allows, that singing Psalms and Hymns was practised in the apostles' days‡ ; and seems to admit that, 1 Cor. xiv. 15. refers to singing in the Church‖. This indeed is undeniably manifest to any one who reads the chapter attentively over. And therefore I take it for granted that our author has no objection to " singing in public worship," if it be performed as it ought to be.

But still he objects against our manner of singing in three or four respects. Against our *joint* singing ; — singing the compositions of other men ; and all sorts of persons singing promiscuously†. And here he objects to *carnal people*, and *women*, joining in the song§§. Before we discuss these several objections separately, I think it may be proper to make one general remark, which I apprehend he will admit the propriety of. It is this. " When any duty is
" enjoined, or any practice recommended both
" in the Old Testament and the New, and no
" command or direction given in the New
" Testament, to vary in the *manner* of perform-
" ing that duty from the manner in which it
" was performed under the Old Testament dis-
" pensation, it is a good and safe method to reason
" from the manner used in the Old Testament to
" that of the New ; and to practise accordingly."
This is admitted, if I mistake not, by Mr. B. and by all considerate men, in many other instances ; and why not in that of singing ? If therefore, Singing have been practised *jointly*,—

C

and

§ P. 11, &c.   ‡ P. 8, 9.   ‖ P. 17.   † P. 9.
§§ P. 18, 19. 29. 37. &c.

and *promifcuoufly* ;—and if perfons have fung the compofitions of *others*, and that with divine approbation ; and if it have formerly been *good, pleafant*, and *edifying* fo to do, and if the bleffed God have never fignified his difapprobation of it in the New Teftament, who has a right to forbid it, or to account it wrong?

FIRST. With refpect then to the firft objection.—Againft "finging with *joint voices*." It is fo manifeft that this was done 'in the Old Teftament Church, that I think none will pretend to deny it. Nor do I recollect that Mr. B. queftions this. Now why fhould there be any change made in the New Teftament church, unlefs we had fome intimation given us that our great Mafter defigned, and appointed fuch a change. But inftead of that, it is at leaft evident, that we have one inftance of this *joint finging* in the practice of our Lord, and his apoftles. Matt. xxvi. 30. Mark. xiv. 26. To fay that, "they " only gave thanks," is to infult common fenfe. Becaufe the word is quite different, and of different fignification from that which is rendered to give thanks‡.—We are likewife juft *before* informed that our Lord had given thanks, and when thankfgiving is mentioned, the word is *fingular*, and applied to our Lord himfelf, and to him alone, as the head of the community ; becaufe he gave thanks in the name of the reft, which is common in all like cafes. But when the hiftorian mentions their *finging*, the word is *plural*; plainly denoting that in this act, the
disciples

‡ ευχαρισησας ver. 27. υμνησανλες ver. 30. in Mat. xxvi. and the fame in ver. 23. 26. Mark xvi.

difciples joined with their bleffed mafter : To difpute a faᵭ fo much crowded with evidence, has the refemblance of petulant obftinacy, in adhering to education prejudices.

Some may poffibly think, that 1 Cor. xiv. militates againft *joint* finging; though I don't remember that Mr. B. has produced any argument againft it from this chapter. But it is very evident, the apoftle is fpeaking of the manner in which the brethren ought to employ their EXTRAORDINARY *gifts*; and not giving rules for their conftant proceeding in their common public worſhip. And more plain ftill, that this chapter cannot be confidered as a directory for the conducting of publick worſhip in following ages, when thefe extraordinary gifts were ceaſed.

SECONDLY. As to " finging *promifcuoufly*." It is not to be denied that this was admitted in the Old Teftament Church ; and if *then*, why not *now*, unlefs forbidden in the New Teftament? I know Mr. B. difapproves of this argument‡. " It is no where forbidden ;" and thinks it fimilar to that of fome weak perfons who argue thus for infant baptifm, becaufe fay they, " it is " no where forbidden." But the cafe is very different. If Baptifm had been a ftanding ordinance under the law, an ordinance from the beginning, and always adminiftered to infants, then undoubtedly the argument of our pœdobaptift brethren would be valid and unanfwerable, For in that cafe, nothing lefs than a divine prohibition could vindicate our refufing

to

to administer this ordinance to infants now.
On the same foundation, it may be incontestibly
argued in favour of promiscuous singing. This
was practised in the worship of the Old Testament. Singing is still enjoined, and no prohibition to sing promiscuously. It therefore unavoidably follows, *cæteris paribus*, that promiscuous singing is right and proper still.

Mr. B. apprehends that promiscuous singing
is wrong on two accounts. " It admits carnal
" people to join in it," " and *women* take their
" part in the service." But we should take
care that we don't set up our own wisdom above
that of God. Carnal people evidently joined
in it formerly.—Carnal people are allowed and
encouraged to attend to, and join in other parts
of divine worship, and why not in this, as well
as the rest ?—Carnal people have often been in-
structed and admonished, and otherwise benefited
in this exercise. Why then should they be deprived
of the opportunity of attending to it ? If it be
a part of *moral duty*, as I think we have proved
it is, then carnal people ought to attend to it,
as well as others. With all deference and submission to so venerable a man as Mr. B. I hum-
bly suppose his objection against this, arises from
two mistaken grounds. A mistaken idea of the
nature and design of singing ; and a mistaken
interpretation of some passages of scripture.

A mistaken idea of the nature and design of
singing in divine worship.—He and many others
seem to conceive of it as if it implied an immediate address to God, arising from present or
past sensations ; and expressive of present or past
experiences. Now to me it appears evident
that

that this is not what is intended by it ; but rather an agreeable and harmonious muſing or ruminating on any ſubject whatſoever, in ſuch a manner as is calculated to ſtrike and engage the mind, and thereby to inſtruct, admoniſh, and edify. And hence, the Pſalms of David, Aſaph, and others, which were ſung in the *Jewiſh*-church, were ſome of them prayers, and ſome of them narrations of facts ; while others were moral precepts, as well as immediate addreſſes of praiſe and thankſgiving to God. The whole book of Pſalms will afford abundant proof of this. Hence David ſays, thy *ſtatutes*,—not thy praiſes only, but thy *ſtatutes* have been my ſongs in the houſe of my pilgrimage. Pſ. cxix. 54. Now why ſhould it not be right and neceſſary for carnal men to ſing theſe ſongs as well as ſpiritual men ?

I think too, that Mr. B has miſtaken the ſenſe of ſome paſſages of ſcripture. I mean, particularly, Epheſ. v. 19—Col. iii. 16. He tells us, " ver. 18. in Epheſ. v. is—the very " ground on which ver. 19. ſtands‡." It is, he ſays, " the very cauſe and reaſon of his bidding them ſpeak to themſelves in pſalms, and hymns, and ſpiritual ſongs," On Col. iii. 16. that " the command to " let the word of Chriſt dwell in them richly in all wiſdom," was that they might be able to continue " teaching and " admoniſhing one another in pſalms, and hymns, " and ſpiritual ſongs§." And he inſiſts that the former part of Col. iii. 16. deſcribes the eſſential qualification for the performance of what

‡ P. 25. § P. 13.

what is contained in the latter part of it†. But he has not, that I can find, given us, nor even attempted to give us the least proof of all this ; nor can I see in what manner he would go about to prove it. It cannot be proved from any thing asserted by the apostle, because we have no such assertion in either of these places. It cannot be proved from any conjunction, or any other connecting words in these verses ; for there are not any such conjunctive or connecting words in either place. The apostle does not say, for instance, in Ephes. " Ye must be filled " with the spirit, that ye may speak to your- " selves, &c." Nor any thing of like meaning or force. And yet if he had said this, it would be no proof that it will always be needful to be " filled with the spirit," in order to sing as here directed, and for the purpose here mention- ed : and that no one must ever sing psalms, hymns, &c. but those who are " filled with the " spirit." To prove this, I mention only one passage, which Mr. B. will allow is, at least, tantamount in signification : It is Acts vi. 3. &c. " Brethren, look ye out seven men—full " of the Holy Ghost, whom we may appoint " over this business." Will Mr. B. say, that none are to be deacons in the church, but those who are, in his sense, " full of the spirit, or of " the Holy Ghost ?" And yet if he chused to assert this, as I believe he hardly will, he would easily deduce proof of it from Acts vi. 3. much more cogent than can be deduced from Ephes. ver. 18, 19, in favor of his interpretation of those verses.

Farther,

Farther, I hope Mr. B. will not undertake to prove what he afferts on Ephef. v. 18, 19, from the two verfes being *joined* in the fame period, and the *order* in which the two claufes ftand. Almoft numberlefs other paffages would demonftrate that this is no proof at all. But if he only read to the end of the period, to ver. 22, he may have full fatisfaction. Will he fay that none *can*, and confequently none *ought* to "give "thanks to God," as ver. 20; or to fubmit "themfelves," as v. 21, unlefs he be filled with the extraordinary gift of the fpirit? I hope not. And yet it is inconteftibly evident, that he has the fame proof of this, as of the affertion I have above tranfcribed from him. I therefore venture to take it for granted, that our author proceeds to his conclufion on miftaken premifes; and that if he had attempted to give fair proof of what he fo pofitively afferts, he would foon have difcovered the fallacy of his own reafoning; and that all he has faid on this paffage, with a view to oppofe promifcuous finging muft unavoidably fall to the ground. And for the fame reafon, we are obliged to draw the fame conclufion refpecting what he fays on Col. iii. 16, which is in the fame ftrain, and built on the fame foundation; and therefore I pafs it by, for the fake of brevity.

After all, I readily grant that ungodly men *do* not perform this, or any other duty as they ought to do, and from a right fpirit. But then, this can never be a reafon why they fhould lay fuch duties afide. Their " *prayer* is abomi- "nation unto the Lord." The very "plowing "of the wicked is fin." But are they, on this
account.

account to lay aside all religious duties, and all civil exercises? And never more regard either the duties of religion or of their calling? Surely not. I think it evidently follows then, that nothing Mr. B. has said, is sufficiently cogent against permitting, and even encouraging carnal men to sing the praises of God.

Yet again, our author still insists *vehemently* insists upon it, that *women* ought not to join in singing the praises of God, in public worship ; and says a great deal indeed, in order to expose this practice, and dissuade from it. I think the whole of what he has said on this subject, that is properly argumentative, is reducible to these two heads : " We have no scripture authority to " encourage women thus to sing." And, " Sing- " ing is speaking, and teaching ; but women " are not to speak or to teach in the church ; " and therefore not to sing."*

As to " scripture authority," if by this be meant, no scripture enjoins in so many words, that " women in public worship, shall join with " men in singing ;" it need not be asserted. Where is it expressly enjoined that women should attend public worship at all? Where are women expressly commanded to sit down at the Lord's table? where we are expressly commanded to preach, or to pray, or to read the scriptures in public worship? I might ask the same questions on multitudes of other subjects : but this would be trifling. I propose these to shew that these requisitions on any subject in dispute, are generally unmeaning and unbecoming

* P. 18——24. and P. 45.

quibbles

quibbles. The bleſſed God conſiders men as poſ-
ſeſſed of rational faculties, and capable of underſtanding the general deſign of his word, without
theſe punctilios of expreſſion in every ſubject.

Women, as well as men have rational capacities ;—they, as well as men, have immortal
ſouls ;—they, as well men, are made for an eter-
nal duration ; they, as well as men, are the crea-
tures of God.—If ſinging the praiſes of God be
a moral duty, which I think has been proved already, they, as well as men, are under an obligation to perform it ;—they, as well as men,
have received many bleſſings from God, which
they ought to praiſe him for.—Conſider ſinging
as proper and uſeful on any ſubject ; praiſe,
prayer, narration, or precept, as we have conſidered it above; women, as well as men, are in-
tereſted in all theſe ſubjects ; they, as well as
men, can underſtand them all ;—and they can
profit by them all. — They, as well men, have
capacities to ſing on them all. They have
the organs of ſpeech, and " the daughters of
" muſick," as well as men.—They can therefore enjoy the advantages of ſinging, and experience the *goodneſs* of it, and the *pleaſantneſs* of
it ; and be edified, and taught, and admoniſhed
by it, as well as men.—Nothing is more common in ſcripture, nor more freely allowed by
grammarians, nor more uſual in language, on
all ſubjects, political, common, and ſacred, than,
to include the woman in the man : and when
directions are given to men, to underſtand thoſe
directions as alſo binding on women. The in-
ſtances are innumerable ; but needleſs to be here
given. The ſcripture, however, ſufficiently inform

forms us that women have joined with men in singing; and that in public worship too: and we have no evidence that the blessed God disapproves of it; but the contrary. *Miriam*, and the Israelitish women joined with Moses, and the rest of the children of Israel. (Exod. xv. i, 20, 21.) Deborah joined with Barak, (Judg. v. 1.) There were singing *women*, among the Jews, as well as singing *men*. Ezra ii. 65. Nehem. vii. 67. The daughters of Heman were under the hands of their father for SONG, and for song IN THE HOUSE OF THE LORD, and for *service* IN THE HOUSE OF THE LORD too, as well as this sons. (1 Chron. xxv. 5, 6.) Women, therefore, have joined in this service; and if the blessed God have never expressed his disapprobation of it, and appointed any change to be made in it, why should they be excluded from it more than men? And why should they be excluded under the New Testament dispensation, more than under the Old?

But singing, says Mr. B. " is *speaking*; and " we are to *teach* by singing. Now women are " not allowed to *teach*, or to speak in the church ; " and therefore not to sing." I venture to answer thus. When women are forbidden to speak or to teach in the church, it must either be understood in the most strict and unlimited sense; it must be understood with some restrictions and limitations; such as the nature of things, the tenor of scripture, and the contexts in question will suggest. Let us examine the subject in both these views.

(1.) Is it to be understood in the most strict and unlimited sense? I apprehend not; for
the

the reasons following.—It is evident that when *teaching* is applied to singing, it is in an unusual and extraordinary sense; not in the sense in which it is commonly understood, as respecting the regular stated worship of God in the church. Now the apostle only forbids women's *teaching* in one single place, 1 Tim. 11, 12. And in that place he is not speaking, that I can perceive, of any thing extraordinary or unusual ; but if he be speaking of public worship at all, which I much question, he is evidently speaking of the ordinary stated worship of the church. Consequently, it is reasonable, and natural to understand teaching there in the common and usual sense. It seems proper, and I think necessary, for women to *speak* in the church on some occasions. For, not here to mention relating experiences, which might possibly excite disputes of another kind, that might divert us from the point in question ; there seems to be a necessity that they should on many occasions give an account of facts in the church, which they alone are acquainted with, and yet are needful to be laid open ; and this they cannot do without *speaking*. — If any false charges are exhibited against women, by which their reputation in the church is any way injured ; or on account of which they are in danger of being excluded ; it seems an intolerable hardship if the women, in such case, be not permitted to vindicate themselves, and clear their characters. but they cannot do this without *speaking*.—If women at any time behave disorderly, and hereby make the church unhappy, or injure its reputation ; it appears to be in this case, highly necessary that the church should examine their
conduct,

conduct, and require them to give an account of it, that it may appear in its own light. And this cannot be regularly done, if women be not permitted to fpeak in the church—If women repent of their conduct, and be ready to give an account of this repentance, they ought to have liberty to do it. But they cannot do this with regularity, and in a fatisfactory manner, unlefs they are permitted to *fpeak* in the church. If any difference arife among women, or between women and other members in the church, when they have taken the previous fteps mentioned Mat. xviii. 15, 16. 17. If thefe prove unfuccefsful, they muft bring the matter before the church. But how can they properly do this, without *fpeaking* in the church? When a church undertakes any thing of peculiar importance or difficulty in which the women may have occafion to be concerned ; or to the expences of which they may have a call to contribute ; or in the good, or bad effects of which, they may be, at leaft, as much interefted as the men are ; it is right they fhould give their voice in it, and their advice concerning it ; and it appears to be intolerant not to allow them this privilege. Befides there may be, and I am perfuaded there are many things which fome of the women underftand better than fome of the men. But they are denied this privilege, and treated in a very intolerant manner, if they be not permitted on any account to *fpeak* in the church. This may be applied particularly, to the admiffion of new members, and the choice of officers, paftors, or deacons in the chuich ; on which occafions, for feveral moft obvious reafons which

need

need not be here mentioned, it is not only right, but even necessary for women to have liberty to *speak*, as well as men.

Yet farther. I think this rule cannot be taken in its most extensive and unlimited sense; for that seems to be inconsistent with some offices which women bore, and some gifts they were possessed of, in the days of the apostles. It is generally granted, if I mistake not, and I think, justly too, that there were *Deaconesses* in [the primitive Church; and that Phœbe, (Rom. xvi. 1) was one of these, and the word *διακονον*, which we render *servant*, seems to imply this. It appears very natural to suppose, that an officer in the church must sometimes have occasion to speak in it. But even this could not be, if the apostle's direction be understood and applied without restriction.—Women in the primitive Church, had certainly the gift of *prophecy*. This was foretold, by the prophet Joel, ii. 28. and commenced on the day of Pentecost. (Acts ii. 16, 17.) The four daughters of Philip had this gift, (Acts xxi. 9.) And this gift was peculiarly exercised in the Church, for the believers, not the unbelievers, 1 Cor. xiv. 22. &c. But they surely could not *prophesy* in the church, unless they *spake* in it. Yet again, the apostle plainly supposes that women did both pray and prophesy in the Church, and gives them directions to do it decently. (1 Cor. xi. 5. &c.) They were then most certainly permitted to *speak* in the church, on some occasions: therefore I conclude that when the apostle "forbids women to speak in the church," he is to be understood with some limitation; and that,

D

2.

2. This limitation muſt be determined, according to the eſtabliſhed rules of interpretation, by " the context in queſtion, the nature of things, and the general tenor of ſcripture. The prohibitions are two ; not to " ſpeak in " the Church," and " not to teach, or to uſurp " authority over the man. The paſſages where they are found are, 1 Cor. xiv. 34, 35. 1 Tim. ii. 11, 12. which I deſire the reader to conſult.

In the former, the apoſtle ſays, " Let your women keep ſilence in the churches : for it is not permitted to them to ſpeak ? &c. I think it is undeniable, from what is ſaid above, that the meaning cannot be unlimited ; that they are never to be permitted to ſpeak in the church, on any occaſion whatever. For that ſeems to be contrary both to the nature of things, and the tenor of ſcripture. In order to judge of the apoſtle's meaning from the *context*, it may be obſerved,—that the apoſtle is enjoining regularity and *order* in the church, ver. 33. Now it is certain there is no diſorder in women joining with men in ſinging the praiſes of God, any more than there is, when *men* jointly ſing his praiſes ; nor more than there is when both ſexes join in prayer. If the divine Being had eſteemed it *diſorderly*, he would have blamed it under the law. But we don't find that he did blame it. Again ; though the apoſtle forbids women to *ſpeak* in the church ; and though, in a ſenſe, we do ſpeak when we *ſing* ; yet ſinging and ſpeaking are very different. Both the name and ſignification differ : and they are always differently underſtood, both in ſcripture, in common life, and in all authors of judgment

and

and credit. Nothing is more plain and certain, or more univerfally known than this. So that no neceffary inference can be drawn from the one to the other.

The *context* will generally be one of the beft *keys* to the meaning of an author. But the context *here,* will by no means authorife us to fuppofe that the apoftle had his eye upon *finging.* Let the paffage be read (1 Cor. xiv. 33, 34, 35.) and it will appear,—(1.) that the injunction is to prevent confufion, and for the fake of order, ver. 33. " God is not the author of confufion, " but of peace." Now it is evident, that when women join with men in finging, there is no *confufion,* nor any thing that tends to the breach of *peace,* more than if only one perfon fing ; or if all the men fing together, and the women remain filent. Women can fing as orderly as men ; and can join in the fong as harmonioufly and as peaceably as men.

(2.) The argument by which the injunction is enforced, has no relation to *finging.* " They " are commanded to be under obedience." (cited from Gen. iii. 16.) But women can be fubject and obedient to their hufbands, and yet join with them in finging. Children are commanded to be obedient to their parents, and fervants to their mafters ; yet Mr. B. will not fay that this is any reafon why a *fon* fhould not join with his *father,* or a fervant with his mafter, in finging the praifes of God ; and therefore the injunction cannot from hence be fuppofed to have any relation to finging.

3. The apoftle prefcribes an *expedient* for women, which fhews that he had no regard to finging, when he enjoins filence upon them. If

they

they would learn any thing fays he, " let them afk their hufbands at home." But to " afk their " hufbands at home," could be no fuccedaneum for *finging*. The one could never compenfate the difadvantage of being prohibited the other. If Paul had faid, " Let them *fing* with their " hufbands at home," we fhould eafily have underftood that he meant, " let them not fing " in the church." And, by parity of reafon, " let them afk their hufbands at home," implies, " let them not afk queftions in the church, to " diforder and difcompofe the church."

(4.) The apoftle, in the laft place, fubjoins, " For it is a fhame for women to fpeak in the " church." But it is plain, from the conftant practice and approbation of it, both in the *Jew-ifh* and *Chriftian* churches, that it is by no means accounted *fhameful* or *indecent* for women to join with men in finging the praifes of God.

On the whole, it appears that the SPEAKING the apoftle forbids in 1 Cor. xiv. is fuch as would be diforderly, and make confufion in the church :—fuch as is fhameful, or *indecent* :—fuch as is contrary to the woman's fubjection to her hufband :—and fuch as will be, at leaft, in a good meafure, precluded, and rendered un-neceffary, by " afking their hufbands at home." I think it is evident that no kind of fpeaking will anfwer this defcription, unlefs it be dictating to the church, and pretending to teach the church, or propofing queftions, to the obftruc-tion of church bufinefs, and the hindrance of its regular proceedings. The *former* is affuming authority over the man ; and they are *both* dif-orderly and indecent. But finging does not
come

come within this defcription ; and therefore does not feem to be in the thoughts of the apoftle.

As to the other text, 1 Tim. ii. 11, 12. though Mr. B. feems to take it for granted that the apoftle has here an eye to public worfhip ; I confefs, I can fee no reafon to admit that he has ; and therefore cannot confider it at all in point to the prefent queftion. But if he will fo underftand it, ftill it has no weight in his favor ; as appears by the confiderations above-mentioned. I have been the more large on this branch of the fubject, becaufe Mr. B. lays much ftrefs upon it.

Thirdly. Mr. B. objects againft " our prac-" tice of finging," that " we fing the compo-" fitions of others ;—and thefe are *human* com-" pofitions ;—and even the compofitions of thofe " we would not chufe to be in church-fellow-" fhip with*." As to finging the compofitions of others, this was conftantly practifed in the Old Teftament church. The book of Pfalms, com-pofed by David, Afaph, and others was ufed for this purpofe; and the pfalms were fent or given to " the chief mufician."to be fung according to the directions fent or given with them. This is clear from many of the titles of the Pfalms. See the titles of Pfalm iv. v.vi. vii. viii. and many others. It is mentioned to the honour of good king He-zekiah, that, among his other excellent attempts to reform the church and nation, " he com-" manded the Levites to fing praifes unto the " Lord with the words of David and of Afaph " the feer."(2 Chron. xxix. 30." There cannot then be any moral turpitude in finging the com-
position

* P. 34, &c.

pofitions of others And did the great God ever appoint a change to be made in this branch of worfhip ? If not, who has a right to forbid, or to alter it now ? *Singing* is as ftriɛtly enjoined in the New Teftament, as it was in the Old, if not more ftriɛtlv ; and we have no command, or direɛtion, that I know of, to fing in a different manner from that in which the Jews performed this fervice.

Still Mr. B. complains that the compofitions we fing are " *human* compofitions ;" that is, not the compofitions of infpired men. Admitting, for a moment, the *criminality* of this. It can only be alledged againft part of what we fing. For a great part of our fongs are the pfalms of David, and others. Thefe are infpired. Mr. B. I think, will not objeɛt, as fome have weakly done, that they are *human*, becaufe they are tranflated into *Englifh*. Nor will he objeɛt, it is hoped, that they are human, becaufe they are *verfe*. He has often heard, that the Pfalms, and fome other parts of the Old Teftament, were written in *Hebrew* verfe. Tranflating them into *Englifh* verfe then, is only modifying them in a proper manner, that they may better refemble what they originally were ; and more completely anfwer the purpofe for which they were originally defigned. And if the perfon who fo modifies them, be judicious and faithful, and give the true fenfe of the facred writers ; they are, at leaft, very nearly, as much a divine compofition as our Englifh tranflation is. And I think, no competent judge will deny, that the facred ardor of the Hebrew poet, which is very effential to good Pfalms and

Hymns

Hymns, may be preferved better in Englifh *verfe*, than in Englifh *profe*.

And if fome other facred fongs be compofed by uninfpired men, on other fubjects; if the truth of fcripture be regarded in them, they are no more *human* compofitions, than our prayers and fermons are. For all our prayers and all our fermons, whether precompofed, or uttered extempore, are, in this fenfe, *human*. And, I own, I could never fee any more harm in a Pfalm or Hymn, than in a prayer or fermon, in this fenfe, compofed by men. It may be faid, the " Pfalms and Hymns are not perhaps, according " to fcripture." The fame may be faid of the prayers and fermons. And who is to be the judge of this? Certainly every man for him-felf. And furely none will fing in the prefence of God, what he believes to be a falfehood. " But one perfon judges of the hymn for the " whole congregation." True; and fo it is in prayer, and preaching. And any one in the congregation has the fame right to reject any part of the Pfalm or Hymn, and to refufe join-ing his voice with the reft in finging it, which he has to refufe joining in a prayer, or receiving the fentiments contained in a fermon, that he ap-prehends to be unfcriptural.

Mr. B. excepts to thefe compofitions, becaufe they are " prefcript, precompofed, and made " ready to our hands*." But if this had been any way improper, furely, we have reafon to believe that our divine Mafter would have blam-ed the Jews for it, or have warned us againft it.

* P. 34. 35, 45, &c.

The

The Jews undoubtedly fung the Pfalms of David and Afaph, " made ready to their hands;" and we have abundant evidence that the great God approved their conduct, and accepted their fervices. And I believe no man can prove that thefe were not the compofitions fung by our Saviour and his difciples at his laft fupper; and by Paul and Silas in the prifon at Philippi; and recommended to the Ephefians and Coloffians; and to fuch as are merry, Mat. xxvi. 30. Mark xiv. 26. Acts xvi. 25. Ephef. v. 19. Col. iii. 16. James v. 13. Indeed there is no neceffity either to prove or to affert that they were fuch. But, if it were needful, I think, much more might be faid for it than againft it.

Mr. B. feems to wonder that we don't ufe precompofed fermons and prayers, as well as precompofed Pfalms and Hymns†. Several reafons might be affigned for this: but I think it fufficient here to fay, we have feen above, that we have Divine Authority for precompofed Pfalms and Hymns; but not for precompofed fermons and prayers. We have alfo a book of Pfalms, provided for us by our great Mafter in heaven; but not a book of fermons and prayers. There is alfo an evident propriety in the reafon of things, to prevent confufion in focial worfhip, in having precompofed Pfalms and Hymns, rather than precompofed prayers and fermons.

Our author feems to *taunt* his " finging breth-" ren," becaufe they bring their Hymns in their *pockets*, to worfhip God‡. But taunts and jeers are light things, and can be eafily borne.

† P. 35, &c.   ‡ P. 8, 26, 35, &c.

However,

However, his " finging brethren" have no def-
picable warrant for this. When He, who is
the fource of wifdom, exhorts his people to worfhip him, he does not bid them *make* a Pfalm,
but *take* one ; plainly fuppofing that it is *made*
ready for them. " Sing aloud unto God our
" ftrength, make a joyful noife unto the God of
" Jacob. Take a Pfalm, and bring hither a
" timbrel ; the pleafant harp with the pfaltery."
(Pfal: lxxxi. 1, 2.) The Lord commanded his
people to *write* a fong for pofterity ; and Mofes
" did fo," (Deut. xxxi. 19, 22.) And David,
the man after God's own heart, " *delivered* the
" Pfalm to thank the Lord, to Afaph and his
" brethren." (1 Chron. xvi. 7.) It is therefore
no new or unfcriptural practice for people to
take Pfalms and Hymns with them to divine
worfhip : and whether we take them in our
pockets or *hands*, or any other way, is a very im-
material circumftance ; and it is hardly confift-
ent with the dignity and the gravity of an aged
minifter of Chrift to treat fuch a circumftance
with ridicule and fneer.

    Once more ; the good gentleman I am en-
gaged with, wonders and mourns, and pities us
very much indeed, that we fhould ufe the compofitions of thofe with whom we cannot unite
in church-fellowfhip†. We anfwer, the reafon
we cannot think it proper to unite in church-
fellowfhip with thofe good men who fprinkle
infants, and do not baptize believers, is not
becaufe we have any difrefpect to their perfons,
or any doubt of their chriftianity, or of their

† P. 34, 35, &c.

knowledge

knowledge of gospel truth, in the chief and fundamental parts of it. But because we apprehend, and firmly believe, that no churches are formed according to the scripture rule, but those which are composed of such members as are baptized on profession of faith in the Lord Jesus Christ.—And we have no rule but that laid down in the scripture.;—and we are not Lords, but servants ; and must act according to the will and direction of our King and Head ; our "Master in heaven." Now as he has given us no authority or licence to join in fellowship with any who are not, as we believe, baptized, our allegiance and subjection to him, require us not to do it. But if any of these good men compose either hymns or sermons, calculated to edify our souls, and agreeable to the truths of the gospel, we see no reason why we may not enjoy the advantage of their labours, as they do of ours, by *singing* their hymns, as well as reading their sermons, or hearing them preach. If we are mistaken in this, we desire to be taught better rather than laughed at, and mourned over. For neither laughter nor lamentation bring any conviction to our consciences.

VII. Being now on the subject, I beg leave, with all due respect and submission to my brethren in the ministry, of every denomination, and the churches under their care, to offer my thoughts freely concerning the *manner* of singing in *christian* churches. As this path is but little beaten, I entreat the candor of the judicious and pious reader ; and venture to propose the following method.

FIRST.

FIRST. To examine the directions of he
New Teftament concerning this practice.

SECONDLY. To attempt anfwering fome
queries, and folving fome cafes of confcience
refpecting it.

THIRDLY. To offer a few general advices,
refpecting the beft manner of conducting it ;
and the chief things to be regarded in it.

FIRST. The directions of the New Teftament. And here we may confider—to whom
they are given—and what they contain.

(1.) To whom they are given. It would be
natural to fuppofe, if we had not full evidence of
it, that thefe directions are given to the *churches.*
The church is " the pillar and ground of the
" truth." (1 Tim. iii. 15.) The great fupport,
under Chrift, of all that God has revealed.
And with whom fhould our bleffed Redeemer
entruft his ordinances, but with his fervants,
his friends, his fpoufe, his brethren ? Such
titles are given to his church, from the different relations in which our Saviour ftands to
his people, and the correfpondent difpofitions
that his people have towards him. None but
thefe have fpiritual underftandings to difcern
what will be moft for his honor, or fpiritual difpofitions to manage his concerns for him. None eife
have a cordial affection for Chrift, that will excite
a holy care for his glory.

And we find that thefe directions are, in fact, given
to the churches, and to members of the churches,
and to them only. Thefe directions are given in
four places. (1 Cor. xiv. Ephef. v. Col. iii. Jam.
v.) All which epiftles are indifputably written to
the churches, and to none elfe. I add, thefe directions

tions are evidently given in general terms, and to all the members of thefe churches without exception. For the apoftles ufe no exceptive or reftraining claufcs, to confine thefe directions to one, more than another. But, as in all other univerfal directions, every one, according to his ability, is under obligation to obferve them. Yet it may be proper to take notice, that (1 Cor. xiv.) relates to extraordinary gifts, both with refpect to finging and other parts of divine worfhip. Thefe are not to be expected at this day : and therefore none can now with propriety attempt to *fing*, any more than to pray, or preach, or prophefy, according to the directions there given. And (Jam. v. 13.) refpects particularly thofe who are merry or chearful. " Is any merry ? Let him fing " pfalms." Yet it cannot be *confined* to him who is *merry*. For if fo, the former claufe would imply that none but the afflicted are to *pray* ; which would oppofe the general tenor of fcripture, and the common fenfe of mankind. But finging pfalms is peculiarly fuited to a chearful difpofition, as prayer is to a ftate of af-fliction. The other paffages (Ephef. v. 19. Col iii. 16.) are quite clear, as to the perfons addreffed in them, and need no comment. It is however manifeft that thofe who have no capacity for finging, cannot be under obligation to practife it, any more than a blind man, can be under obligation to read and " fearch the " fcriptures." And the fame may be faid of every other general command contained in the bible. I venture to recommend it to thofe who are incapacitated to fing, that they *breathe* after

the

the fingers, or take fuch other methods as they may find moft ufeful, in order to keep their mind attentive to the fong, and to the matter contained in it. And, in doing this, whatever mere idle fpeculation may fuggeft, I know from good evidence, that the fpiritual fongs of the church, will be far from being unprofitable even to thefe.

There are others, whofe capacities, both of voice and ear, are very flender; yet there is in them a foundation for improvement, though a weak one. And it has been afferted by good judges, and fkilful teachers, that thefe, by labour and diligence may make a confiderable proficiency. Thefe, therefore, ought to improve the fmall capacity they have, for the honor of God, the edification of the church, and their own advantage. And this is as evidently proper and requifite, as it is for a preacher to learn to fpeak well, that he may *preach* to the greater advantage of the people.

2. What do thefe directions contain? Here we may obferve, that Mr. B. takes much pains to expofe " our prefent way of finging; and feems to infift upon it, that becaufe we cannot prove it fcriptural, in all the various circumftances of it, we ought to lay it afide. And this appears to be the chief defign and object of his tract. But I beg leave to afk him, Can he vindicate by plain fcripture, his *manner* of praying or preaching? Can he by plain fcripture vindicate that method of conducting public worfhip which is adopted by any party, or any particular church in Great Britain? I freely confefs, I cannot. What then? Muft prayer, and preaching, and all public worfhip be laid afide? It is evident, if Mr,

E

B's

B's arguments be valid enough to annul the practice of finging, they are equally fo to annul the practice of praying and preaching; and to demolifh the whole fabric of publick worfhip all together. The cafe appears to be this. The great God has condefcended to give us *general* rules with refpect to finging, preaching, and praying, fufficient for the edification of his church. But he has not given us *particular* rules with refpect to mode and form, and other circumftances in any part of public worfhip. And, as Chriftian churches are fo different, in capacity, fituation, and other circumftances, it appears to be a great proof of divine Wifdom and goodnefs that fuch particular directions are not given; as we cannot fee how they could have been given, without reducing Chriftianity to a ftate of bondage, like that of the Jews. Surely Mr. B. knows that finging is *differently* practifed in different congregations. And the fame is true of *praying* and *preaching*, and it is requifite that it fhould be fo for the reafons above hinted at. And yet it is very poffible that all thefe different ways of finging, praying, and preaching may be equally fcriptural, becaufe no *particular directions* are given; and they may all be equally conformable to *general* rules; of which we fhall fpeak hereafter. Perhaps, if our author would confider thefe plain things, he would fee the impropriety of calling "our practice of finging" by fo many ugly names.

3. We return to the Directions; which relate to the *matter* of our fongs;—the *ufe* and *defign* of finging;—and the *manner* of conducting it.

As to the *matter* of it; we are directed to
fing

fing " Pfalms, and Hymns, and fpiritual fongs."
There is confeffedly a difficulty in fixing the
precife meaning of thefe words, and determining
the exact *difference* of their fignifications. Yet
this need not create any hefitation refpecting
the practice; for on every poffible interpretation, the injunction retains its force ; and the
direction is fufficiently plain, for the purpofes
defigned. It may be proper, however, to obferve what the learned have faid on thefe
words.

PSALMS in the New Teftament, evidently
fignifies that part of Scripture commonly called
" the Book of Pfalms." This is clear from
Luke xx. 42. xxiv. 44. Acts i. 20. xiii. 33.
Nor do I know of any imaginable reafon why
we fhould underftand it differently here. And
therefore, when we are finging any part of the
Book of Pfalms, we are not deviating from the
rule. Yet the different compofures in the
Book of Pfalms have not all the fame title.
Some are entitled *Songs*, the very word we have
in the texts now in queftion. And the title of
the 145th Pfalm is a word which feems moft
naturally to fignify praife, and to be equivalent
to *Hymn*. And the fame *Hebrew* word is the
running title of the Book of Pfalms. Hence
fome imagine that by Pfalms, Hymns, and
fpiritual Songs, the Apoftle intends the feveral
compofitions contained in the Book of Pfalms.
While others apprehend that the Apoftle here
directs us to fing, either David's Pfalms, or
the Songs of good men, compofed before that
time, as of Zacharias, Simeon, and others. Or
any that might be compofed in that very age,
by thofe who had gifts for the purpofe.

For it is a known fact that Hymns and Spiritual Songs, were compofed in the early ages of the Chriftian Church ; whether fo early as the Apoftle's time or not. Others explain the words thus. " Pfalms are fuch compofures as contain exhortations to holinefs and good conduct ; Hymns thofe which celebrate the praifes of God, for the benefits we have received from him. Songs, thofe which teach us the doctrines of truth, &c||. How juft foever this interpretation be, the Book of Pfalms is an inconteftible proof, that thefe are all proper fubjects for facred fong; and confequently, that finging is not defigned to be a direct and experimental addrefs to God. But that perfons may profitably fing in divine worfhip, on fubjects in which they have no immediate concern. I have ftated this matter in this familiar way, that, if poffible, the moft fimple reader may form fome fatisfactory conceptions of it. On the whole, it appears clear to me, from thefe paffages, and from what has been faid above, that any Pfalm, or Hymn, or Spiritual Song, that is founded on fcripture, and confiftent with it, though not in its very words, may be as properly, and as profitably ufed in divine worfhip, as any prayer or fermon, though ever fo fcriptural, which is not in the very words of fcripture. Nor am I able to conceive a reafon why perfons fhould be confined to the language of fcripture in finging, more than in prayer or preaching.

4. Thefe directions relate to the ufefulnefs and defign of finging in the worfhip of God.
It

|| Vid. Liegh in verb. υμνος, & Polum in loc.

It is evident from Col. iii. 16. that this practice is defigned for inftruction and admonition. Thefe pfalms, hymns, and fpiritual fongs, contain truths, narrate facts, recommend duties, relate experiences, and reprove and threaten finners, in a manner fuited to give this inftruction and admonition. This is admirably clear in the pfalms of David, to every attentive reader. While thefe are fung, the melody raifes the fpirits, and excites pleafure, whereby the contents of the fong, more eafily engage the attention, and affect the heart ; and the inftructions more agreeably infinuate themf.lves into the mind, I believe, I may truly fay, that this is always, in a degree, the cafe with thofe who fing with attention.

Yet here it is queftioned whether this inftruction and admonition be *mutual* ; i. e. whether a number of perfons finging together can be fuppofed hereby to inftruct and admonifh *one another*. Mr. B. pofitively denies that in finging together, and finging the compofitions of others, we teach and admonifh at all. " You " neither teach yourfelves," he fays " nor any " body elfe§." But I don't fee any great force in his reafoning on this head. I think it is not unufual, in common language, to fay that we teach or admonifh others, when we repeat to them what others have faid or written, as well as when we fpeak from our own knowledge or experience.—And if the pfalms which the churches were directed to fing, were the pfalms of David, which is the meaning of the

E 3   fame

§ P. 243

ſame word every where in the New Teſtament, and therefore moſt reaſonably ſo underſtood here; then it is certain the churches did ſing what was precompoſed by others, for inſtruction and admonition among themſelves. Conſequently, it is certain, that ſinging precompoſed forms, is perfectly conſiſtent with teaching, ſo underſtood. And if the words in Col. iii. 16. be expreſſive of *mutual* teaching, then this practice is undeniably conſiſtent with teaching mutually, or " teaching one another.

I ſay, " if the words be expreſſive of *mutual* " teaching ;" for though this is generally taken for granted, I cannot help doubting it†. I confeſs I am never fond of ſeeing the original referred to, and the common verſion changed in order to gain a point; though it may give light to a ſubject on ſome ſpecial occaſions. However, left Mr. B. ſhould think I wiſh, in the preſent caſe, to take an advantage of him, I will beg leave to relate a ſimple fact, which, I hope, he will not aſcribe to oſtentation ; and

leave

---

† Good Mr. Rees, in his Pamphlet on Singing (p. 29.) ſpeaking of the Greek word εαυτους, uſed Col. iii. 16. ſays, " If the word be fairly examined, it denotes *mutuality*; or it neceſſarily implies doing a thing mutually, from one ſide to another." Leigh, on the other hand, underſtands the *text*, in the common way : yet differs from Rees, as to the meaning of the *Greek Word*. His ſalvo is, εαυτοις pro αλλη λοις uſurpatur, Epheſ. iv, 32. & εαυτους pro αλληλους, Col. iii. 16," But neither of them gives proofs, only refers to Epheſ. iv. 32: And I ſubmit it to the genuine Critic, whether the ſentiment be not too eaſily taken for granted, by Expoſitors in general.

leave him and the reader to draw the conclufion.

When I was carefully confidering thefe two
paffages, Ephef. v. 19. Col. iii. 16. I was ftruck,
as I have been before, to find the fame pronoun
rendered in Ephef. v. 19. " yourfelves," and in
Col. iii. 16. " one another." Upon this, I re-
folved deliberately to examine the Greek Teftament on the fubject. The refult is, unlefs I
have counted or judged wrong, that I find the
fame word ufed two hundred and feventy-three
times; and there are only four places, befides
the two in queftion, in which there is even the
appearance of *mutuality*. The four places are,
Ephef. iv. 32. Col. iii. 13. Heb. iii. 13. 1 Pet.
iv. 10. and how far it is abfolutely neceffary
to underftand the word as denoting mutuality
in thefe places, I fhall at prefent fubmit to thofe
who are capable judges. But certainly, if the word
in Col. iii. 16. be capable of another interpretation, one would not wifh to explain it in a manner different from the general fignification of it.

I grant, that " teaching and admonifhing
yourfelves," is a little uncouth : but " fpeak-
" ing to yourfelves," Ephef. v. 19. and " com-
" fort yourfelves" 1 Thef. v. 11. are nearly as
much fo. With thefe hints, however, fimple as
they are, I leave the fubject to thofe who have
leifure and inclination to confider it more mi-
nutely. And, for the prefent, I venture to give
it as my own opinion, that not *mutual*, but *perfonal* inftruction and admonition are defigned by
finging, and intended in Col. iii. 16.

5. Refpecting the *manner* of finging. Here a
few general remarks may deferve regard. (1.)
We

We have no particular directions given in the New Testament, that I remember, for the *manner of conducting* any part of divine worship. The New Testament is, in this, as well as in other respects, a " a law of liberty ;" Our blessed Saviour perfectly knew that his followers would be attended with such a variety of differing circumstances as might, in many cases, make it very inthralling to be tied up to *particular rules* ; and therefore in his wisdom and love, he has not done it. Many wife and gracious purposes appear to be hereby answered. Now, as we have no particular direction given us with regard to any part of publick worship. it is no wonder we have none concerning the *manner* of singing. Nevertheless, we have sufficient *general* directions concerning every part of worship, and singing among the rest. (2.) It is very plain we have authority in the New Testament for *joint* singing, from the example of our Lord and his disciples, (Mat. xxvi. 30. Mark xiv. 26.) And it is most natural and reasonable, as all men must allow, to understand Acts xvi. 25, as an example of it.—But it is clear that a person may sing to advantage, and in a manner that is pleasing to God, when no other joins with him. James v. 13. " Is ANY merry, (or chearful, " ευθυμει) let him sing Pfalms."——I add, that we learn from 1 Cor. xiv. that this, as well as other parts of divine worship, was performed in an *extraordinary* manner. But this cannot be a rule for other churches, or for after ages to be *confined* to ; because then it would follow that all divine worship must be laid aside when extraordinary gifts ceased; which I

hope

hope none will be defperate enough to aſſert. Thus it appears that we have clear authority for *joint*, for *feparate*, and for *extraordinary* finging in the New Teſtament. (3.) We cannot, I think, learn with certainty, whether the directions given in Eph. v. and Col. iii. relate to public worſhip or no. To me it appears that they may juſtly be applied to any of the cafes abovementioned. For whether the whole church be aſſembled, or only two or three ; or a perfon be alone; in all theſe cafes, we may " ſpeak " to ourſelves," and " teach and admoniſh our- " felves in Pſalms, and Hymns, and Spiritual " Songs."

The *general* directions concerning this and every other part of divine worſhip, are ſuch as theſe, " Let all things be done to *edifying*." 1 Cor. xiv. 26. " Let all things be done *decently* and in " *order*," ver. 40. " Whatſoever ye do, do all " to the *glory of God*." 1 Cor. x. 31. " Let all " your things be done with *charity*." 1 Cor. xvi. 14.

It is evident, at firſt fight, that theſe general rules are to be applied to all that is done in the church of Chriſt, and in the worſhip of God, and ought to be religiouſly kept in view in the performance of all, by every one concerned. But to enlarge particularly on the full import and intention of all theſe rules, would lead me far beyond my intended brevity.—And the *glory cf God*;—the *edification* of our fouls in know- ledge, faith, comfort, and holinefs ;—*decency* and *order* ; ſo as that every thing may obtain the ap- probation, as much as poffible, of every wife, thoughtful, and good man ; and harmony and
love

love; that no mind may be hurt, no one's fpirit embittered, no one deprived of his advantages ; no one's affections alienated from any of his brethren ;—thefe, I fay, are fuch eafy phrafes, and the ideas conveyed by them fo obvious, and fo commonly underftood by every church of Chrift ;—and can be fo readily illuftrated by every minifter, and almoft by any of the brethren, that there feems to be nothing requifite, but that our minds be properly influenced by the fear and love of God, in order to put them in practice. I may juft obferve, however,

1. That all thefe *general* directions are moft evidently given to the church, and to every member of it without exception ; and to none but thofe in church fellowfhip: and confequently all who are in church fellowfhip have a right, and are under the ftrongeft obligation to fee that they be attended to ; and to give all the affiftance they can in putting them in practice. And none can be clear before God, who does not obferve them ; though it is evident that thofe who have moft underftanding, and moft influence in the church, are culpable in a peculiar degree, if they neglect them.

2. They all admit of variety, according to the different circumftances of churches, and of individual members. This is the cafe in finging, preaching, and prayer ; and in almoft every other branch of worfhip. The fituations, the capacities, the difpofitions, and even the prejudices of different individuals, *may*, and I think *ought*, to have fome influence here, in order that thefe general rules may be all regarded, and kept in view. In preaching, for inftance, the
fame

fame kind of addrefs, the fame ftyle, the fame method of handling a text ; that would fuit and profit one church, would be unfuitable and un- profitable to another. The inftances by which this might be illuftrated, are almoft numberlefs. It is alfo the cafe with refpect to *finging*. Some churches are well improved and far advanced in the knowledge and practice of it ; and are fitu- ated among thofe, who, in general, underftand it well. Some are directly the contrary. Now it is beyond a doubt with me, that one method of finging would be *edifying*, would tend to *love* and *harmony*, would be *orderly* and *decent*, in one of thefe churches, and yet would be quite different, and have a quite different effect in the other. And cafes of this kind are eafily multi- plied by every minifter, and by every man of confideration and judgment; and applied to every branch of worfhip. Mr. B. indeed fays, " All the churches did undoubtedly obferve one " and the fame method of carrying on and per- " forming the feveral parts of publick wor- " fhip§." But he has given us no proof of the truth of this affertion. And if he mean with refpect to *mode* and *form*, that they all fung and preached, and prayed exactly in the fame me- thod, I am perfuaded it is both unfcriptural and unreafonable to fuppofe any fuch thing. We can find no method prefcribed to all the churches, and therefore there was no method needful to be thus univerfally attended to. The capacities of minifters, as well as of people, will hardly admit of it. The directions mentioned above,

and

§ P. 26

and many others, suppose a difference in these and all other indifferent matters ; and therefore imply, that they did not in all things follow the same method. Their different circumstances would render the same method impracticable, consistent with observing the rules abovementioned. And therefore, it cannot, I think, be rationally supposed, that they were exactly confined to the same method. This leads me to observe,

3. That these *general* directions require close consideration, and wise and serious consultations in every church of Christ ; in order to be persuaded that they do worship God in that *manner* which is, on the whole, best calculated to answer these noble ends, and conformable to these rules ; that is, that all things be " done to edi-" fying,—decently, and in order,—to the glo-" ry of God,—and with charity." Singing, praying, and preaching are all strictly enjoined, are all proper exercises for seasons of publick worship; and have all, as far as we can learn, been attended to in publick worship in all ages. But we have no particular rules for the *manner* of performing any one of these exercises, that I can recollect. And therefore, the rules abovementioned are to be religiously kept in view ; and every minister, and every church evidently ought to consider all the circumstances of the whole community, so far as possible, and apply the rules to the circumstances, and act accordingly.

4. As no plan is calculated for general good, which may not in some instances, be against the taste, or interest of individuals ; it may be so in
this

this cafe, after all that is done to make the finging, or any other part of worfhip, as generally agreeable and profitable as may be. When it fo happens, then is the time to practife thofe duties of *fubmiffion* and *fubjection* one to another, which are required of all the members of churches, which particularly fuit thefe circumftances; and which are fo amiable, ufeful, and honourable, wherever they are practifed. " Ye " younger fubmit yourfelves to the elder ; " yea all of you be fubject one to another ; " and be clothed with humility." " Submit " yourfelves one to another, in the fear of " God‡." And where this care is taken, and thefe duties practifed, there is no great danger of any thing being done materially wrong ; or any part of divine worfhip being performed in a manner that is difpleafing to God ; or, on the whole, unprofitable to men. I proceed,

SECONDLY. To attempt the folution of fome difficulties, or cafes of confcience, that appear important to fome perfons, refpecting the *manner* of finging.

1. Is it right to fing *Anthems* or Songs in profe, in public worfhip ?

I anfwer, however profitably a fingle perfon, or a few perfons together may fing thefe, I cannot think them a proper part of the *public* worfhip of Almighty God ; for fuch reafons as the following.—All the members of churches are directed to join in finging, as we have feen above ; and it is evidently incumbent on them, fo far as they can. But few can join in the

‡ Ephef. v. 21: 1 Pet. v. 5.

F
           fing-

finging of *Anthems*; nor have they fufficient time or fkill to learn them. And therefore, if Anthems be fung, many of the brethren will generally be deprived of their privileges, and of an opportunity of doing their duty in the worfhip of God. One capital rule is, "Let all "things be done to edifying." But, however it may pleafe the ear, experience fhews that the finging of Anthems is not fo edifying to the foul, as Songs in verfe, that are fet to plain tunes.—The Pfalms and Songs contained in Scripture, for the ufe of the Old Teftament Church, were wrote in *verfe* ; which is, at leaft, a tacit admonition not to fing in *profe*, and a proof that finging in profe, in the worfhip of God is unfcriptural.—We have no evidence that Chrift, or his apoftles, or the primitive church, ever fung *Anthems*; but good evidence that it took its rife in the fourth century, when the church was filling with corruptions, and popery was faft advancing towards its height§. —This, and all *antiphonal* finging, generally prevents many from the advantage and pleafure they would otherwife have in divine worfhip, and has generally been the foundation of fetting up a *choir* of fingers, many of them vain and carnal, to perform the worfhip of the church-members, whofe right it is ; and thus many of the members either perform not this worfhip at all, or they do it by *proxy*, which is vile in the extreme. And I fhould be glad to know why we may not pray, and receive the Lord's fupper

§ Peirce's Vindication of Diffenters, Part iii. p. 101. &c. Tans'ur's Elements of Mufic difplayed, p. 190.

by

by proxy, as well as fing by proxy; and why carnal people might not as well perform every other duty for us, as fing for us?—And that this practice deftroys the folemnity, and fpirituality of divine worfhip is too manifeft to need a formal proof. Many other evils naturally follow, and have in fact followed this way of finging, which, for the fake of brevity I here pafs over. But they would all be prevented, if finging were confidered, as it ought to be, as *peculiarly* the bufinefs of the church; and if it were performed with that *gravity* and *fimplicity* which are always requifite in religious matters, and which are the two chief glories of Chriftianity.

Q. 2. Ought Organs, and mufical Inftruments to be ufed in Chriftian Worfhip?

I anfwer, I am perfuaded they ought not; for—they are not once mentioned in the New Teftament which is the chief directory of Chriftians—And it is certain they were not introduced into the church till Popery had nearly arrived to its height. Even Bellarmine himfelf does not pretend that they began to be ufed fooner than A. D. 660. And there is good reafon for fuppofing that they were far from being even fo early as that age†. And, to me it is wonderful that any who fear God, can give countenance to them.

Q. 3. Is it right to learn to fing by Notes?

I anfwer; To me it appears quite proper, and laudable, for thofe who have time and capacity for it. For—It is plain the Jews taught

Pe irce ut fupra. p. 106, &c.

this

this regularly, as other arts are taught. 1 Chro.
vi. 31. xv. 22. 27. 2 Chron. xxiii. 13.—
Singing muſt be performed " decently, and in
order." Nothing can be ſo done, that is not
done *properly*. Nothing can be done *properly*
that is not properly learnt. And the Notes
moſt properly teach to ſing with exactneſs and
propriety.—Singing without *harmony* is moſt
evidently indecent and diſorderly. There cannot be harmony unleſs there be uniformity of
voice, and found : and to obtain this uniformity,
nothing can be more advantageous than to have
the Tune exactly pricked in Notes, and learnt
from them.—A tune is nothing more than a
collection of founds properly modified and pro-
portioned to each other, which is learnt by the
poſition and form of the Notes. Theſe founds
may undoubtedly be learnt, with conſiderable
exactneſs by the *ear*. But every one acquainted
with ſcience well knows, that what is learnt
both by *eye* and *ear* at the ſame time, is learnt
with moſt eaſe, and to greater perfection.—
And there is clearly the ſame reaſon why a
ſinger ſhould learn to ſing by rules and notes,
as there is for a preacher to have learnt the
rules of Grammar, Logic, and Rhetoric, to
enable him to ſpeak properly, to reaſon juſtly,
and to addreſs mankind in an agreeable manner. And no man of underſtanding can diſpute
the propriety of this in a preacher. Yet I beg
leave here to ſuggeſt, to prevent altercations
and impoſitions in the church ; that though
learning to ſing by pricked notes is evidently
proper and laudable, in thoſe who have opportunity; yet this is by no means abſolutely *neceſſary*

fo

for all who join in finging. Becaufe—it·is no where commanded in fcripture.—And it is a known fact, that perfons can learn to fing with fufficient exactnefs by the ear. Many can fpeak with tolerable propriety without learning Grammar by written rules ; can reafon juftly enough for common purpofes, without reading a fyftem of Logic; and can inftruct and perfuade forcibly and agreeably, without making themfelves mafters of a Treatife of Rhetoric. I therefore conclude, that it would be well for all to learn the Notes, who can do it conveniently and confiftently with other duties and engagements ; and that thofe who cannot, fhould unite with the brethren and affift each other as well as they are able, and all harmoniously join together in finging to the glory of God.

Q.4. Ought *carnal* people, or our own *children*, to join with us in finging the praifes of God ?

Anf. To me it is clear that they ought. For,—confider finging as a *natural* action ; they are, in this view, as capable of performing it as others.—Confider it as a part of worfhip, and a *moral* duty, as prayer and hearing are, which, I think, has been already proved ; in this view, it is binding on all men, converted and unconverted.—Confider the advantages to be received from it; *inftruction* and *admonition*. They ftand in need of thefe, and are capable of receiving them, through the blefling of God, as well as others ; and we know that fome unconverted perfons have received them in this part of worfhip.—Many places in the Pfalms, exhort *all* men to fing to the Lord, and to fing his praifes. —The objection, that " they don't experience " what they fing" has no weight at all, as we

F 3

have

have feen before, becaufe that is unneceffary, from the very defign of finging.

Q. 5. Is it right to fing in parts? And if fo, in how many parts?

Anf. I know of no fcripture, nor any rational argument, which militates againft finging in parts, admitting it be done in *love*, and appear to be moft for the fpiritual *edification* of the church,—and fuppofing that upon mature confideration, it evidently appear to be moft for the *glory of God.*—It cannot be denied that different voices will *beft* fuit different parts : and this, feparately confidered, may be allowed to be a plaufible argument in favor of finging in parts. Yet this argument is by no means decifive; becaufe it is well known that thofe who can fing the other, efpecially the higher parts, can generally join in the Tenor.—Singing in parts, whether more or fewer, is a matter of choice ; and I think all men will acknowledge, that thofe who fing in one part only, fing as *properly*, though not as *melodioufly* as thofe who fing in many. And if this, upon ferious examination, fhould be found more to the edification of the church, this edification will be a rich compenfation for defect in point of melody. — Becaufe generally, the greateft part in moft churches, have not fuch fine fenfations, nor are fo enamoured with the fineft melody; as fome others are. Yet thefe plain fouls, (admit the expreffion) are to be edified, as well as the reft. When this is confidered, perhaps it will appear that the fimpleft and plaineft manner of finging will anfwer the beft end in moft churches. Singing in *two* parts, is

I think

I think, moſt generally practiſed in Chriſtian Churches; and in my opinion, it generally is the moſt profitable. But wherever it becomes a ſubject of controverſy, there moſt evidently ought to be a ſerious conſultation; and as it is a matter of mere choice, every member in the church has a right to give his voice and be heard upon it. The edification of all is to be regarded, and their voices, their diſpoſitions, and ſenſations muſt be all tenderly examined, and the practice ſettled and regulated accordingly.

Q. 6. Who ought to be chiefly conſulted, and moſt regarded in chuſing the *Tunes* that ſhall be ſung in divine worſhip, if this be debated in the church?

Anſ. All undoubtedly ought to judge what is right, and to reaſon concerning it, according to the general Rules we have ſo often referred to. But there are frequently ſome who are fond of finer Muſick and can profit by it too; while others cannot join in it, becauſe they cannot underſtand it; and therefore cannot profit by it. Now in this caſe, and in every other, where indiſpenſable duty does not bind, " We that are ſtrong ought to bear the infir- " mities of the weak, and not to pleaſe our- " ſelves. Let every one of us pleaſe his neigh- " bour, for his good to edification. For even " Chriſt pleaſed not himſelf." Rom. xv. 1, 2, 3.—Reaſon and common humanity require this. For thoſe who can be profited by finer and more difficult muſic, can be profited alſo by the plain and eaſy; and they can edify themſelves at *other times*, by ſinging Pſalms in Tunes which are

be-

beyond the capacities of many of their brethren. It therefore looks cruel and inhuman to sing those tunes when their weaker brethren ought to join with them.—Consider the order of well-regulated families. In these, whatever belongs to real business, and to the interest of the parents or of the family in general, those children who are arrived at understanding and strength of body are charged to take the care of; and however disagreeable to the infants, this must be done. But whatever is merely circumstantial, and, according to the family phrase, " sig-" nifies little or nothing," the *children* must be pleased in this; and those who are grown to understanding must deny themselves. This family order is founded in nature, and there is every reason for observing it in the church of God.—Yet all ought to remember, that nothing is to be done in the church merely for the *plea-sure* of Individuals; but the *edification* of the whole. 1 Cor. xiv.

Q. 7. Ought unconverted persons, who are not in church fellowship, to have *authority* in managing or directing this part of Christian worship?

Ans. We undoubtedly may, and ought to oblige even these, so far as we are able, consistent with the " edification of the body of Christ." And this ought to be done in preaching, prayer, and every other part of worship. But certainly they ought not to have any such authority, as that mentioned in the Query. For—these are generally young persons; and therefore cannot be supposed to have examined things of this kind; or to be qualified to judge what is right
and

and wrong, as perfons who have authority, or take the lead in divine worfhip ought to be.—They are too commonly *unfteady* in their tempers and more led by fancy than truth ; fo that giving *authority* to thefe, is like committing the direction of a fhip to an unfkilful pilot ; the confefequences of it may be fatal.—Befides, thefe not being converted, or " led by the Spirit of " God," cannot be fuppofed to be fo truly confcientious in confulting the edification of the whole church, as all who direct the worfhip of it ought to be.—Again, *experience* is one of the beft helps in directing divine matters for univerfal edification: but edification fuppofes a *foundation laid*, of which thefe have no *experience* ; and therefore the *authority* now in queftion is inconfiftent with their character and ftate.—Farther, fuch people are not only *ignorant*, but frequently *obftinate* too; and unwilling to be controlled, and fet right, when they are wrong. And fuch a temper as this utterly difqualifies any man for authority and direction in divine matters. Even a *minifter* muft not be *felf-willed*. Tit. i. 7.—Once more, they neither have, nor (as unconverted) can have that fenfible and fympathetic attachment to the interefts of the church, and of the weak and ignorant in it, which is abfolutely neceffary in directing divine worfhip; that fuch directors may be excited to zeal, felf-denial, and refolution, in ftudying, and labouring to promote the fpiritual welfare of the whole church.—And laftly the directions concerning finging, are not given to thefe, as we have feen above ; but to churches, and members of churches.

It

It may be thought I have have been too minute in the foregoing remarks. But the ftate of fome churches, and the views of fome perfons, appear to me to afford a fufficient apology. And for the fame reafon, I fhall venture,

THIRDLY. To mention a few fuch remarks and *rules*, as I think will be naturally collected from what has been faid ; and, if I miftake not, will be found agreeable both to reafon and fcripture : though I only mention them, and leave the reader to judge of their propriety and importance.

1. It is plain, that finging the praifes of God is an effential duty, and an important part of Chriftian worfhip, ftrictly enjoined in both Teftaments ; which nothing but incapacity can juftify the neglect of ; and that general edification is the great object of it.

2. It is a duty enjoined on the church in *general* ; and in the New Teftament, on the church *alone* : though it is plain, from the nature of things, and from the Old Teftament, that others have a right to join in it ; and that they may do it to great advantage.

3. In order that the fong may be general throughout the whole congregation, as it ought to be, it is requifite that fuch tunes be fung, and fuch only, as the members in general can join in. I cannot fee how we can juftify a perfon who leads the fong, in fixing upon a tune generally unknown, better than we can juftify one who *preaches* or *prays* in an unknown tongue. And though it be right that new tunes be introduced, yet they ought to be learnt at another time, and not in divine worfhip. For the fcience of mufic,

and

and the art of finging can have no more to do with this part of divine worfhip, than the art of grammar, rhetorick, or logic, have to do with preaching or praying. But learning thefe arts is work for another feafon, than that of divine worfhip; and therefore, fo is learning the tunes that are to be fung in the houfe of God.

4. That the members of the church have all the authority and rule in their own hands, in whatever relates to this or any other part of divine worfhip: and that unconverted perfons be not left to direct what tunes fhall be fung, or the manner of finging them. Becaufe the *edification* of the church, and the glory of God, are the great objects to be attended to; and unconverted people have not capacities to attend to them: for they are "fpiritual things," to be "fpiritually difcerned," and cannot be underftood by the "*carnal* man."

5. That thofe members, who have capacities for this part of Chriftian worfhip, make it their endeavour, by notes, or by the ear, to be able to join in it with concord and harmony, that all things may be. "done decently and in order." For though there is no neceffity for *fine* finging, any more than *fine* praying or preaching; yet there is the fame neceffity that finging be performed with propriety and harmony, as there is that thofe who pray or preach fhould ufe propriety of fpeech.

6. That unconverted people, and the children of the members of churches be not only *permitted* but *encouraged* to join in the exercife; that they alfo may receive inftruction and admonition by it.

7. The

, 7. That the capacities, and all other circumstances of every church be seriously considered
among themselves; and that such parts, and so
many parts be sung, as, upon careful examination of the matter, will appear most likely to
answer the great end of general edification;
" that all our works may be done with charity."

8. Above all: Let every one remember, that
whatever is done profitably and acceptably in
religion, must be done seriously. Let the *heart*
be engaged. " Sing with the Spirit." Let
the *mind* be employed. " Sing with the understanding." Melody must be " made in our
" hearts to the Lord; and we must " sing to
" the Lord with grace in our hearts;" and in
doing this, may expect his presence and approbation, through Jesus Christ.

Thus I have dropped a few thoughts freely,
though briefly, " on SINGING in the Worship
" of GOD." May He " who inhabits the
" praises of ISRAEL," command his blessing on
those who read them!

THE END.

ERRATA.